BRITISH RAILWAYS STEAMING IN THE SOUTH WEST

Compiled by
PETER HANDS

DEFIANT PUBLICATIONS
190 Yoxall Road
Shirley, Solihull
West Midlands

Printed on behalf of Richard Netherwood Ltd., by Gorenjski tisk d.d., Slovenia

CURRENT STEAM PHOTOGRAPH ALBUMS AVAILABLE FROM DEFIANT PUBLICATIONS

VOLUME 14
A4 size - Hardback. 96 pages
-178 b/w photographs.
£14.95 + £1.50 postage.
ISBN 0 946857 40 7.

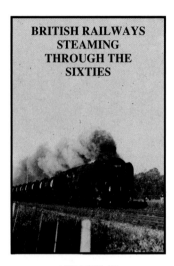

VOLUME 15
A4 size - Hardback. 96 pages
-178 b/w photographs.
£16.95 + £1.50 postage.
ISBN 0 946857 52 0.

A 'VALEDICTION'
A4 size - Hardback. 96 pages
-173 b/w photographs.
£19.95 + £1.50 postage.
ISBN 0 946857 64 4.

VOLUME 1
A4 size - Hardback. 96 pages
-177 b/w photographs.
£14.95 + £1.50 postage.
ISBN 0 946857 41 5.

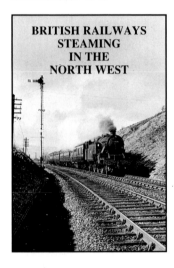

A4 size - Hardback. 96 pages
-174 b/w photographs.
£18.95 + £1.50 postage.
ISBN 0 946857 60 1

A4 size - Hardback. 96 pages
-177 b/w photographs.
£19.95 + £1.50 postage.
ISBN 0 946857 62 8.

VOLUME 11
A4 size - Hardback. 96 pages
-176 b/w photographs.
£16.95 + £1.50 postage.
ISBN 0 946857 48 2.

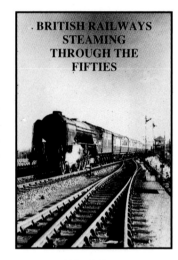

VOLUME 12
A4 size - Hardback. 96 pages
-176 b/w photographs.
£16.95 + £1.50 postage.
ISBN 0 946857 49 0.

VOLUME 1
A4 size - Hardback. 96 pages
-177 b/w photographs.
£14.95 + £1.50 postage.
ISBN 0 946857 39 3.

VOLUME 1
A4 size - Hardback. 96 pages
-174 b/w photographs.
£14.95 + £1.50 postage.
ISBN 0 946857 42 3.

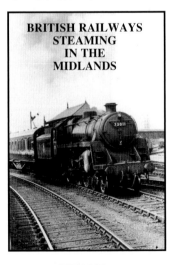

VOLUME 2
A4 size - Hardback. 96 pages
-177 b/w photographs.
£19.95 + £1.50 postage.
ISBN 0 946857 63 6.

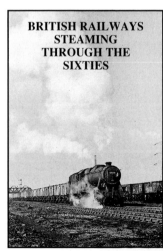

VOLUME 16
A4 size - Hardback. 96 pages
-178 b/w photographs.
£18.95 + £1.50 postage.
ISBN 0 946857 61 X

CURRENT STEAM PHOTOGRAPH ALBUMS
AVAILABLE AND OTHER TITLES

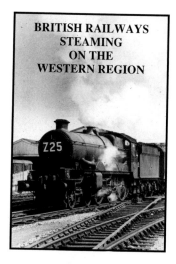

VOLUME 4
A4 size - Hardback. 96 pages
-177 b/w photographs.
£15.95 + £1.50 postage.
ISBN 0 946857 46 6.

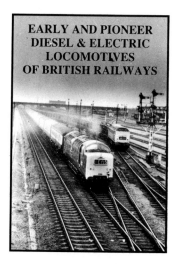

A4 size - Hardback. 96 pages
-177 b/w photographs.
£15.95 + £1.50 postage.
ISBN 0 946857 45 8.

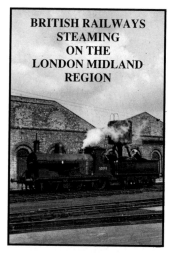

VOLUME 4
A4 size - Hardback. 96 pages
-177 b/w photographs.
£15.95 + £1.50 postage.
ISBN 0 946857 47 4.

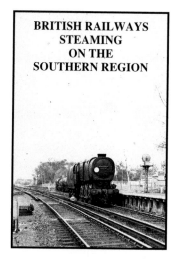

VOLUME 3
A4 size - Hardback. 96 pages
-177 b/w photographs.
£17.95 + £1.50 postage.
ISBN 0 946857 54 7.

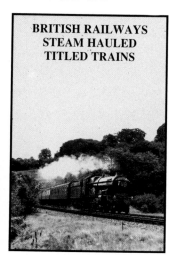

A4 size - Hardback. 96 pages
-169 b/w photographs.
£16.95 + £1.50 postage.
ISBN 0 946857 51 2.

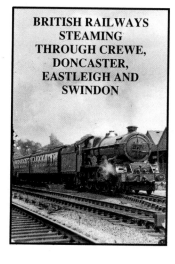

A4 size - Hardback. 96 pages
-179 b/w photographs.
£17.95 + £1.50 postage.
ISBN 0 946857 53 9.

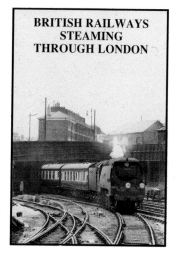

A4 size - Hardback. 96 pages
-174 b/w photographs.
£17.95 + £1.50 postage.
ISBN 0 946857 55 5.

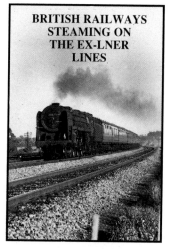

VOLUME 4
A4 size - Hardback. 96 pages
-183 b/w photographs.
£17.95 + £1.50 postage.
ISBN 0 946857 57 1.

'50th' ALBUM
A4 size - Hardback. 96 pages
-186 b/w photographs.
£16.95 + £1.50 postage.
ISBN 0 946857 50 4.

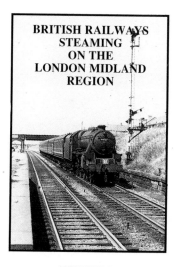

VOLUME 5
A4 size - Hardback. 96 pages.
- 177 b/w photographs.
£17.95 + £1.50 postage.
ISBN 0 946857 58X.

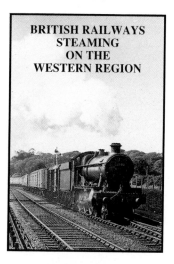

VOLUME 5
A4 size - Hardback. 96 pages.
- 177 b/w photographs.
£17.95 + £1.50 postage.
ISBN 0 946857 59 8.

COMEDY
269 pages. Cartoons.
£9.95 + £1.00 postage.
ISBN 0 946857 30 X.

ACKNOWLEDGEMENTS

Grateful thanks are extended to the following contributors of photographs not only for their use in this book but for their kind patience and long term loan of negatives/photographs whilst this book was being compiled.

T.R.AMOS TAMWORTH	B.W.L.BROOKSBANK MORDEN	N.L.BROWNE ALDERSHOT
R.BUTTERFIELD MIRFIELD	R.S.CARPENTER BIRMINGHAM	KEN ELLIS SWINDON
J.D.GOMERSALL SHEFFIELD	B.K.B.GREEN WARRINGTON	P.HAY HOVE
JOHN HEAD EASTBOURNE	R.W.HINTON GLOUCESTER	F.HORNBY NORTH CHEAM
A.C.INGRAM WISBECH	ALAN JONES BATH	D.K.JONES MOUNTAIN ASH
DENIS LEWIS TEIGNMOUTH	T.LEWIS *	ERIC LIGHT TICKHILL
TERRY NICHOLLS BRISTOL	T.B.OWEN CAEMELYN	R.PICTON WOLVERHAMPTON
N.E.PREEDY GLOUCESTER	J.SCHATZ LITTLETHORPE	JOHN SMITH LENS OF SUTTON
G.H.TRURAN GLASTONBURY	A.WAKEFIELD DRONFIELD	D.WEBSTER *
B.WILSON SOLIHULL		

* Courtesy of the Norman Preedy collection.

Front Cover - Shadows encroach upon the railway scene in the Luxulyan Valley in deepest Cornwall on a bright summer's day on 1st August 1953 as 83E St. Blazey based GWR 5700 Class 0-6-0PT No 8733 steams towards a distant signal (at caution) with a Newquay branch line local passenger train consisting of three carriages. Withdrawn from St. Blazey shed in February 1962, No 8733 was scrapped two months later at Swindon Works. (R.S.Carpenter)

ISBN 0 946857 62 8

(C) P.B.HANDS 1998
FIRST PUBLISHED 1998

INTRODUCTION

BRITISH RAILWAYS STEAMING IN THE SOUTH WEST adds yet another dimension to the wide variety of albums produced from within the 'Defiant Publications' stable.

This album contains a large variety of different locations and locomotives and the author hopes the reader will have his recollections of the South West of England rekindled. Many of the railway locations portrayed are long gone, including the much loved and long lamented former Somerset and Dorset route from Bath to Bournemouth.

These books are designed to give the ordinary, everyday steam photographic enthusiast of the 1950's and 1960's a chance to participate in and give pleasure to others whilst recapturing the twilight days of steam.

Apart from the main 1950's and 1960's series, further individual albums like this one will be produced from time to time. Wherever possible, no famous names will be found nor will photographs which have been published before be used. Nevertheless, the content and quality of the majority of photographs selected will be second to none.

The majority of photographs used in this album have been contributed by readers of Peter Hands series of booklets entitled "What Happened To Steam" and "BR Steam Shed Allocations" (both still available) and from readers of the earlier "BR Steaming Through The Sixties" albums. Under normal circumstances these may have been hidden from the public eye for ever.

If you require any further information about the availability of the books in the 'Defiant Publications' range, please contact:-

Tel. No.
0121 745-8421

Peter Hands,
190 Yoxall Road,
Shirley, Solihull,
West Midlands B90 3RN

Peter Hand

CONTENTS

CHAPTER

PAGES

ONE   BRISTOL-PENZANCE   6–43

TWO   SALISBURY-PADSTOW   44–75

THREE   BATH-BOURNEMOUTH   76–93

FOUR   LAST RITES   94

MEMORIES OF THE SOUTH WEST AREA
OF BRITISH RAILWAYS

1) Pinhoe station, Exeter in August 1964. (Alan Jones)

2) Halwill station, looking east on 28th June 1960. (N.L.Browne)

3) Exeter St.Thomas station on 6th May 1963. (J.Schatz)

4) Axminster signalbox on 30th August 1964. (Alan Jones)

5) Barnstaple (Victoria) station in April 1964. (N.L.Browne)

CHAPTER ONE - BRISTOL-PENZANCE

6) We commence our journey at Bristol, gateway to the Western Region section of the south west area of BR from the Midlands and the north, where, at Temple Meads station on 31st August 1963, the fireman of 84A Wolverhampton (Stafford Road) based GWR *Castle* Class 4-6-0 No 7014 *Caerhays Castle* hurries back to his footplate after affixing the lamps to the brackets of his charge. *Caerhays Castle* is in charge of a Penzance to Wolverhampton (Low Level) express. (J.Schatz)

7) Sporting an express headcode, BR Class 4 4-6-0 No 75008, from 86C Cardiff (Canton), lifts its safety valves as it waits impatiently for the 'off' at Temple Meads with a passenger train in 1957. In October 1958, No 75008 was drafted to 81F Oxford where it remained for several years during which time it acquired a double chimney (September 1962). Prior to condemnation in December 1965, No 75008 also served from the sheds at Templecombe, Exmouth Junction and Worcester. (D.K.Jones)

8) Looking the worse for wear, locally based (82B St.Philip's Marsh), GWR *County* Class 4-6-0 No 1024 *County of Pembroke* rounds the curve near to Bath Road bridge and drifts into Temple Meads with the 5.25pm local passenger train from Taunton on 30th August 1962. *County of Pembroke* had arrived in the Bristol area (82A Bath Road) in June 1958 from 84K Chester (GWR). It left 82B in October 1963, moving to a final abode at 82C Swindon from whence it was withdrawn in April 1964. (R.Picton)

9) Despite it being a soaking wet and thoroughly miserable looking day on 17th March 1963 there is much admiration for the sleek lines of LNER A4 Class 4-6-2 No 60022 *Mallard* (34A Kings Cross) as it simmers at the head of an enthusiasts special at Temple Meads. This world famous locomotive was withdrawn from service the following month from 'The Cross' and after a lengthy period of storage at Doncaster Works it was eventually restored to its former glory. (R.Picton)

10) A gaggle of spotters mill around one of the platforms at Temple Meads as GWR *Castle* Class 4-6-0 No 5053 *Earl Cairns*, from 83A Newton Abbot, takes on fresh water supplies whilst in charge of a westbound express on 13th September 1955. *Earl Cairns*, in spotless external condition, departed from 83A for pastures new at 83D Laira (Plymouth) in November 1959. A final transfer in September 1961 took it to 88A Cardiff (Canton), being condemned from there in July 1962. (D.K.Jones)

11) Designed by G.J.Churchward the GWR 4700 Class 2-8-0's, built between 1919 and 1922, only ever numbered a total of nine units and were employed in the main on express freights to the west of England and between Paddington and Birkenhead. When used on passenger traffic they were mighty useful locomotives. On 30th September 1962, No 4707, of 81C Southall, is employed at Temple Meads with a 'Somerset & Dorset' special organised by the Locomotive Club of Great Britain. (N.E.Preedy)

12) Apart from the many passenger turns seen at Temple Meads there was also an abundance of freight traffic. With the footplate crew looking towards the camera, GWR *Grange* Class 4-6-0 No 6829 *Burmington Grange*, from 83A Newton Abbot, heads a partially fitted freight bound for the west on 7th September 1958. Constructed at Swindon Works in March 1937, *Burmington Grange*, a maid of all work, survived in service until November 1965, being withdrawn from 85A Worcester. (N.L.Browne)

13) With a tank engine in attendance, GWR *Hall* Class 4-6-0 No 6904 *Charfield Hall* is almost ready to return to its home base at Stourbridge with an express at Temple Meads on a gloomy 5th March 1961. For many years an 84E Tyseley engine, *Charfield Hall* was transferred to 83A Newton Abbot in August 1959, but was returned to the Midlands in February 1960, firstly to 84G Shrewsbury and then to 84F Stourbridge later the same year. Its final base was at 84C Banbury. (D.K.Jones)

14) Conversation time at Temple Meads station between the driver and fireman of locally based GWR 5101 Class 2-6-2T No 4139 as their charge is watered on an unknown day in 1953. Keeping No 4139 company is an unidentified GWR 0-6-0PT. No 4139, drafted to 85D Kidderminster and 85B Gloucester (Horton Road) in March and July 1957 respectively, was one of the first examples of the 41xx series to be withdrawn, from 85B in July 1958, being cut up at Swindon later in the year. (D.K.Jones)

15) The main passenger traction depot in Bristol was at Bath Road (82A) situated within a stone's throw of Temple Meads station. Constructed in 1934 it boasted a ten-road running shed along with a small repair shop. Closed to steam on 11th September 1960 it was then converted into a diesel depot. Shortly before closure to steam one of its inmates, BR Class 3 2-6-2T No 82042, is noted near to the depot on 20th August 1960. After closure, No 82042 was transferred to 82E Barrow Road. (B.Wilson)

16) 82B St.Philip's Marsh, often referred to as 'SPAM', a large twin turntabled roundhouse, took over the mantle of most steam hauled passenger workings after Bath Road closed and continued to do so until complete closure in June 1964. On 9th June 1961, GWR *Castle* Class 4-6-0 No 7016 *Chester Castle* is a visitor to 82B from 87G Carmarthen. *Chester Castle* spent most of its working life based at depots in Wales, being condemned from 88L Cardiff East Dock in November 1962. (D.K.Jones)

17) We venture westwards from Bristol and our first port of call is at Yatton where the roof of the station sports some crude, but presumably effective ventilation lights. GWR 4500 Class 2-6-2T No 5535 (82A Bath Road) pauses with a three-coach stopper bound for Bristol on 3rd July 1955, near to an elderly gentleman, hands in pockets, who is standing near to an advertising hoarding. No 5535 was withdrawn from Bath Road shed in June 1957 and scrapped at Swindon. (F.Hornby)

18) A member of the footplate crew of LMS Class 2 2-6-0 No 46525, of 82B St.Philip's Marsh, leans precariously out of his cab as he reaches for the single line token at Yatton station whilst in command of a freight working on 17th February 1962. For many years an 82B steed, No 46525 was ousted from the depot eight months after this picture was taken, moving to 89A Shrewsbury. After condemnation in December 1964 it was despatched to Cashmores, Great Bridge. (Terry Nicholls)

19) We join the main line from Paddington at Taunton, some 145 miles from the nation's capital. Possibly substituting for a more powerful locomotive, GWR *Hall* Class 4-6-0 No 4914 *Cranmore Hall*, another St.Philip's Marsh steed, is in charge of *The Devonian* and proudly carries the headboard of the same on 6th August 1959. *Condover Hall* remained on the books at St.Philip's Marsh shed up until withdrawal in December 1963. It was later scrapped at Birds, Risca in 1964. (A.Wakefield)

20) During the latter years of its existence the branch line from Taunton to Barnstaple was almost the exclusive preserve of the surviving members of the GWR 4300 Class 2-6-0's based at Taunton shed (83B). In March 1964, some six months before the branch died, No 5336 is noted at Barnstaple with a three-coach local passenger. Along with No 5336 (withdrawn in September 1964), surviving sister engines based at 83B were Nos 6326/45/63 and 7303/20/32/37. (N.E.Preedy)

21) GWR 4300 Class 2-6-0 No 7319, from 83B and in original condition, with no outside steampipes, is seen travelling light engine at Barnstaple Junction station on 24th June 1960. This loco, built in 1922, has brought a train round from the original terminus at Victoria Road and having run forward from the same is now passing through the up platform before retiring to the local shed to await its next Taunton bound local. It was condemned in October 1964. (N.L.Browne)

22) We return to the West of England main line at Tiverton Junction where GWR 4500 Class 2-6-2 Tanks Nos 4555 and 4591 have been seconded from 83E St.Blazey and 83D Laira (Plymouth) respectively to haul a special over the Tiverton branch on 24th February 1962. They are noted in tandem after completing their journey. No 4555 was withdrawn from Laira in November 1963 for preservation. No 4591, condemned in July 1964 from 82C Swindon, was scrapped. (G.H.Truran)

23) On a dull 9th May 1963, GWR 1400 Class 0-4-2T No 1471, from 83C Exeter St.Davids, propels the 7.10pm local passenger from Dulverton to Exeter out of Tiverton station which was doomed to closure the following year. No 1471, once of 86D Llantrisant and 86A Newport (Ebbw Junction), had arrived at St.Davids shed in September 1958. It was taken out of revenue earning service from 83C in October 1963 and cut up at Swindon Works the following month. (J.Schatz)

24) We continue our westward journey and pause for a while at Exeter St.Davids station, where, on 29th June 1950, GWR 4500 Class 2 2-6-2T No 5525 is employed on an Exe Valley local passenger train. From January 1957 up until withdrawal in September 1962, No 5525 was employed at four different depots -82A Bristol (Bath Road), 83F Truro, 83B Taunton and 83A Newton Abbot. After lengthy storage at Swindon it was despatched to a South Wales scrapyard. (R.S.Carpenter)

25) With steam to spare 81A Old Oak Common based GWR *Castle* Class 4-6-0 No 4075 *Cardiff Castle* arrives at Exeter St.Davids station on 8th September 1961 with the 8.45am express from Bristol (Temple Meads). Despite looking in fine external condition this January 1924 built locomotive was destined to be condemned from 81A two months after this photograph was taken after covering 1,807,802 miles. It was scrapped at its birthplace, Swindon, in March 1962. (R.Picton)

26) In common with most of the steam locomotives housed at the sheds in Devon and Cornwall, GWR *Grange* Class 4-6-0 No 6836 *Estevarney Grange* looks well cared for as it awaits departure from St.Davids station with the northbound *Devonian* on 24th April 1957. No 6836, an inmate of 83A Newton Abbot, was reallocated to 83D Laira (Plymouth) in May 1960. Further transfers took it to 86G Pontypool Road and 85A Worcester where it died at the latter in August 1965. (Denis Lewis)

27) The vast majority of the mighty GWR *King* Class 4-6-0's allocated on a regular basis to 83D Laira (Plymouth), Nos 6004 *King George III*, 6008 *King James II*, 6010 *King Charles I*, 6017 *King Edward IV*, 6021 *King Richard II*, 6025 *King Henry III*, 6026 *King John*, 6027 *King Richard I* and 6029 *King Edward VIII*, were ousted from the depot by September 1959. On an unknown date in 1955, No 6015 is ready for the road at St.Davids with a Paddington to Newquay express. (R.W.Hinton)

28) Up until closure to steam in October 1963 there had been a motive power depot adjacent to St.Davids station since 1894. In BR days the four-road running shed was coded 83C and had a mixed allocation of locomotives. On 1st September 1952, GWR *Hall* Class 4-6-0 No 4954 *Plaish Hall*, a local inhabitant, is noted in the yard in bright sunshine. On the occasion of the author's last visit on 29th April 1962 there were in excess of thirty steam engines on shed. (D.K.Jones)

29) We return to the West of England main line and skirt the Exe estuary at Starcross on a sun-filled 20th September 1954. GWR *Castle* Class 4-6-0 No 5071 *Spitfire* (83A Newton Abbot) speeds towards the camera with *The Cornishman* express. Originally named *Clifford Castle* (a name later carried by No 5098), No 5071 was renamed *Spitfire* during September 1940. Equipped with a double chimney in May 1959, No 5071 was withdrawn from 82B St.Philip's Marsh in October 1963. (N.E.Preedy)

30) WD Austerity Class 8F 2-8-0 No 90224, allocation not known, emerges into bright sunshine from a tunnel near Dawlish and heads westwards with a partially fitted freight during the first summer of nationalisation in 1948. Records show us that by January 1957, No 90224 was an Eastern Region locomotive shedded at 40B Immingham. Later transfers took it to 36E Retford, 36A Doncaster and finally to 41J Langwith Junction from whence it was condemned in March 1964. (D.K.Jones)

31) Looking fresh from overhaul at Swindon Works, GWR *Castle* Class 4-6-0 No 5050 *Earl of St.Germans*, from 84G Shrewsbury, has a good head of steam as it passes the sea wall at Teignmouth with the 8.00am express from Plymouth to Crewe on 2nd August 1956. No 5050 was yet another member of the *Castle* Class to change names, from *Devizes Castle* in August 1937. Its final abodes were at 81A Old Oak Common and 82B St.Philip's Marsh and was withdrawn from the latter in August 1963. (T.Lewis)

32) GWR *Castle* Class 4-6-0 No 5011 *Tintagel Castle*, an 83A Newton Abbot steed, accelerates away from the Teign estuary with an express in the summer of 1955. *Tintagel Castle* was ousted from Newton Abbot shed by diesel traction in May 1960, moving to 81D Reading. Five months later and No 5011 was on the move again, this time to a final home at 81A Old Oak Common. Constructed in July 1927 it was condemned in September 1962 after covering some 1,732,65 miles. (D.K.Jones)

33) Newton Abbot is our next port of call and in circa 1956 the station platform is deserted as locally based (83A) GWR 1400 Class 0-4-2T No 1466 simmers gently with the stock of an auto-train bound for the Moretonhampstead branch line (closed to passenger traffic during 1959). No 1466, transferred to 83C Exeter St.Davids in April 1961 and 83B Taunton in October 1963, was withdrawn from the latter in December 1963 and today is preserved at GWS Didcot. (R.S.Carpenter)

34) With a GWR 4-6-0 type for company, a usurper from the Southern Region, Unrebuilt *West Country* Class 4-6-2 No 34027 *Taw Valley* (72A Exmouth Junction) graces Western Region metals at Newton Abbot with the 12.30pm stopper to Plymouth on 24th April 1957. In common with No 1466 in the above frame, *Taw Valley* was also destined for preservation. Taken out of traffic from 70E Salisbury in August 1964 it was stored at Barry Docks from January 1965 until February 1980. (Denis Lewis)

35) GWR *Castle* Class 4-6-0 No 5056 *Earl of Powis* has been neglected by the cleaning staff at 81A Old Oak Common as it poses for the camera at Newton Abbot during the bad winter of 1962-63. *Earl of Powis*, possibly substituting for a failed diesel, is in charge of a down postal which was running very late due to the extreme weather. During the last year or so of its working life, No 5056 was allocated to the sheds at Cardiff East Dock, Hereford and Oxley. (G.H.Truran)

36) Rebuilt in 1926 from GWR *Star* Class 4-6-0 No 4037 *Queen Philippa, The South Wales Borderers*, newly transferred to 83A from 87E Landore (Swindon), is photographed at Newton Abbot on a local passenger turn in July 1957. The auther has a childhood memory of spotting this 'rarity' at Birmingham (Snow Hill) in the late fifties - a 'rarity' which just had to be 'cabbed'. Drafted to 83C Exeter St.Davids in July 1962, No 4037 was condemned two months later. (Eric Light)

37) At its height Newton Abbot boasted a locomotive shed and workshop situated within the near vicinity of the station. On a dull day on 14th August 1960 there is a quite busy scene near to the entrance to the depot where we espy several engines awaiting their next call to duty, including GWR *Castle* Class 4-6-0 No 5003 *Lulworth Castle* and GWR 5101 Class 2-6-2T No 5154, both being native to 83A. *Lulworth Castle* was taken out of revenue earning traffic in August 1962. (R.S.Carpenter)

38) Sporting the headcode '555', GWR *King* Class 4-6-0 No 6014 *King Henry VII*, which retained its 'V-shaped' cab roof from its semi-streamlined days right up until withdrawal from 84A Wolverhampton (Stafford Road) in September 1962, reverses out of the shed yard at 83A Newton Abbot to take up an express working on 22nd August 1953. *King Henry VII* was modified with a double chimney in September 1957. The depot lost its links with steam traction in August 1962. (N.L.Browne)

39) Aller Junction, the control point for the lines to Kingswear and Plymouth, witnessed a steady stream of trains in steam days and it was not until the eighties that it lost its semaphore signalling. The next six photographs are dedicated to those now far-off halcyon days. Travelling bunker-first, GWR 5101 Class 2-6-2T No 6166 (83A Newton Abbot) powers an eight-coach Torquay bound local in August 1959. The following month No 6166 was drafted to 83D Laira. (Eric Light)

40) Another Newton Abbot steed, GWR *Castle* Class 4-6-0 No 4098 *Kidwelly Castle*, passes the same location at Aller Junction and heads towards Dainton bank and Plymouth with a down express in August 1959. Rendered surplus to operating requirements by the shed hierarchy at 83A in July 1962, *Kidwelly Castle* was reallocated to 81A Old Oak Common. It remained at 81A until condemnation in December 1963 and was eventually scrapped at Cashmores, Great Bridge in June 1964. (Eric Light)

41) GWR *King* Class 4-6-0 No 6017 *King Edward IV*, from far-off 84A Wolverhampton (Stafford Road), passes a row of sentinel-like lineside telegraph poles at Aller Junction as it coasts towards Newton Abbot in August 1959. *King Edward IV* is in charge of a Plymouth to Paddington express. Remaining on the books at Stafford Road until condemnation in July 1962, No 6017 was cut up at Cox & Danks, Langley Green, Oldbury in May 1963 after a period of storage at 84A. (Eric Light)

42) Appearing to be doing all the donkey work, 83D Laira (Plymouth) based GWR *King* Class 4-6-0 No 6004 *King George III* surges towards the camera at Aller Junction as it pilots an unidentified GWR *Castle* Class 4-6-0 with a down express in August 1959. The following month *King George III* took its leave of Laira shed, moving to 81A Old Oak Common. It finished its lengthy career at 86C/88A Cardiff - Canton (August 1960-June 1962) and was scrapped at Swindon. (Eric Light)

43) Another 'double-header' at Aller Junction, this time in the summer of 1957. GWR *Grange* Class 4-6-0 No 6842 *Nunhold Grange*, from 82B St.Philip's Marsh, pilots an unknown GWR 4-6-0 as they head westwards towards Plymouth on a level gradient. The grade will soon alter as they head for the fearsome Dainton bank. *Nunhold Grange* had a brief sojourn at 83G Penzance, from January to April 1962, before returning to 82B. It was condemned from there in November 1964. (Eric Light)

44) We take our leave of Aller Junction with a third 'double-header'. Under clear signals, GWR *Hall* Class 4-6-0 No 6938 *Corndean Hall*, of 83A Newton Abbot, pilots an unidentified *Modified Hall* Class 4-6-0 as they charge along with an express in August 1959. Three months on and *Corndean Hall* found a new home at 83D Laira. Prior to being rendered surplus to operating requirements in March 1965, No 6938 also served from 81D Reading and 81E Didcot. (Eric Light)

45) We break off from our westward journey to Plymouth and beyond by visiting the Torbay branch, where, during the heydays of steam traction, thousands of holidaymakers with their buckets and spades travelled by train to the seaside resorts in this part of Devon. In the summer of 1958 two unidentified GWR types double-head a northbound express out of Torquay station. In the distance a BR Class 3 2-6-2T waits at signals with a Newton Abbot to Kingswear local passenger. (R.S.Carpenter)

46) Looking in fine external fettle apart from a stained front end, GWR 5101 Class 2-6-2T No 4150 (83A Newton Abbot) lifts its safety valves as it departs from Torquay station with a local working from Newton Abbot to Kingswear in August 1959. No 4150 was drafted to 83C Exeter St.Davids from May 1960 until July 1961 after which it returned to 83A. It took its leave of the Devon area for good in July 1962, transferring eastwards to 82D Westbury. (R.S.Carpenter)

47) Paintwork gleaming, GWR *Castle* Class 4-6-0 No 5079 *Lysander* looks every inch a pedigree as it glides towards Paignton station with an express on a sun-filled 27th July 1956. Constructed at Swindon Works in May 1939 shortly before the outbreak of the Second World War, No 5079 was originally named *Lydford Castle*. It was renamed *Lysander* in November 1940 and was one of the first members of the class to be withdrawn - from 83A Newton Abbot in May 1960. (D.K.Jones)

48) Heavy foliage abounds on the hillsides on the approach to Kingswear on a dull day in August 1959. GWR 4300 Class 2-6-0 No 7311 (83C Exeter St.Davids) skirts the banks of the river Dart as it steams towards the small terminus with a five-coach down local passenger. The sight of steam hauled suburban trains at this stage of time was soon destined to disappear as diesel multiple units tightened their grip. No 7311 was condemned from 83C in September 1962. (Eric Light)

49) Another August 1959 scene. With a badly scorched right side cylinder, GWR *Manor* Class 4-6-0 No 7806 *Cockington Manor* is wedged up against a wooden bufferstop at Kingswear station as it awaits turning prior to setting off homewards to Newton Abbot with a return working. No 7806 departed from 83A the following month, moving to 83E St.Blazey. Its last years were spent working from sheds in the Midlands, namely 84E Tyseley, 84F Stourbridge and 84B/2B Oxley. (R.S.Carpenter)

50) We return to the West of England main line and focus our attention for a while on the awesome Dainton bank, between Aller Junction and Totnes. The gradients from Aller run for some two and a half miles, at best 1 in 46 and at worst, 1 in 36. On a dull summer's day in 1957, GWR *Castle* Class 4-6-0 No 7035 *Ogmore Castle*, from 82A Bristol (Bath Road), steams along with the up *Cornishman* express from Penzance to Wolverhampton (Low Level). (Eric Light)

51) With the sun beating down, GWR *Manor* Class 4-6-0 No 7813 *Freshford Manor*, of 83D Laira (Plymouth), struggles up Dainton bank with a loose-coupled mineral train on 12th June 1958. Giving assistance from the rear is GWR 5101 Class 2-6-2T No 5108 which was withdrawn from 83A Newton Abbot the following month. *Freshford Manor* later served from the depots at 83F Truro, 85A Worcester, 84E Tyseley, 81D Reading, 82C Swindon, 85B Gloucester (Horton Road) and 81E Didcot. (D.K.Jones)

52) Looking in magnificent external condition, SR Unrebuilt *West Country* Class 4-6-2 No 34106 *Lydford*, from 72A Exmouth Junction, churns out white smoke a'plenty as it powers a Plymouth to Exeter (Central) passenger train on Dainton in the summer of 1959. Built in March 1950, *Lydford* spent many years at 71B Bournemouth before being transferred to Exmouth Junction in January 1958. It was condemned from 72A/83D in September 1964 after only fourteen years of service. (Eric Light)

53) Remaining in the summer of 1959, twin exhausts are heard on Dainton as GWR *Grange* Class 4-6-0 No 6873 *Caradoc Grange*, an 83D Laira (Plymouth) steed, pilots an unidentified GWR *Hall* Class 4-6-0 past an instruction notice with a heavily loaded express. Apart from a very brief period spent at 83G Penzance, No 6873 remained at Laira until May 1962, moving to a final home at 82B St.Philip's Marsh. Withdrawn from there in June 1964 it was cut up at Swindon during 1965. (Eric Light)

54) Maximum effort at Dainton summit as the exhausts from two steam locomotives reverberate off the banks of the cutting. In bright sunshine the pioneer member of the GWR *Grange* Class 4-6-0's, No 6800 *Arlington Grange* (83G Penzance), pilots a GWR *Hall* Class 4-6-0 with an express bound for Newton Abbot and beyond in the summer of 1953. *Arlington Grange* was ousted from Penzance shed by the ever increasing ranks of diesel-hydraulic locos in July 1962. (R.S.Carpenter)

55) A down express bound for Plymouth emerges from the 272 yards long Dainton tunnel in the summer of 1953. Assisting the train engine, a GWR *Castle* Class 4-6-0, is GWR *Hall* Class 4-6-0 No 5920 *Wycliffe Hall*, of 83A Newton Abbot. *Wycliffe Hall* remained at Newton Abbot shed until May 1961, moving to a new abode at 83B Taunton. In September of the same year it was drafted to a final home at 82D Westbury where it was rendered surplus to operations in January 1962. (R.S.Carpenter)

56) Far from its home base at 82A Bristol (Bath Road), GWR 4500 Class 2-6-2T No 5553 drifts along bunker-first with a train of vans near to Totnes station at the foot of Dainton bank, some 202 miles away from Paddington on 30th July 1958. Five months later and No 5553 found itself in mid-Wales at 89C Machynlleth where it remained until November 1960, returning to the south west at 83E St.Blazey. After many years of storage at Barry it was saved for posterity. (R.W.Hinton)

57) No sooner has Dainton bank petered out when the next obstacle, Rattery bank, appears. Nine miles long at gradients of 1 in 60 and 1 in 46 it finally eases to 1 in 90 at Tigley church. On 18th August 1952, GWR *Manor* Class 4-6-0 No 7805 *Broome Manor* pilots GWR *County* Class 4-6-0 No 1010 *County of Caernarvon* (83D Laira - Plymouth) with an express. Of these two fine locomotives, No 1010 was withdrawn in July 1964, followed by No 7805 in December of the same year. (D.K.Jones)

58) 83D Laira (Plymouth) shed, opened in 1901 on filled ground on the south side of the main line, was some fifty minutes walk away from Plymouth (North Road) station. In this photograph, taken on 10th March 1963, its steam allocation had been much reduced in number thanks to the ever increasing arrivals of diesel traction. In steam in the yard are GWR *Modified Hall* Class 4-6-0 No 7924 *Thornycroft Hall* and GWR *Hall* Class 4-6-0 No 5939 *Tangley Hall*. (J.Schatz)

59) A crowded scene within the confines of Plymouth (North Road) station on 20th April 1960. Locally based (83D Laira) GWR 6400 Class 0-6-0PT No 6413 is in charge of the 6.15pm local passenger working to Saltash. Once of 86J Aberdare and unusually 14D Neasden on the London Midland Region, No 6413 had been at Laira since October 1959. This sturdy locomotive soldiered on at 83D until condemned in November 1961 after which it was scrapped at Wolverhampton Works. (R.Picton)

60) Departing westwards from Plymouth, GWR *Grange* Class 4-6-0 No 6824 *Ashley Grange*, from 83G Penzance, skirts the shoreline at St.Budeaux whilst in charge of a Penzance bound parcels train on Sunday 29th April 1962. *Ashley Grange*, one of a numerical trio of such engines based at 83G at this stage in time, left the shed for good in August 1962, briefly being allocated to 83D Laira before moving on to pastures new at 81E Didcot and 81F Oxford. (D.K.Jones)

61) Having crossed the Royal Albert Bridge and then the viaducts at Coombe, Forder, Wiveliscombe, Noltar and Tiddy and traversing the depths of the tunnel at Shillingham we find ourselves at St.Germans, where, on a misty 14th June 1954, GWR *Hall* Class 4-6-0 No 6911 *Holker Hall*, of 83E St.Blazey, heads an express through wooded countryside. *Holker Hall*, transferred to 84C Banbury in November 1959, finished its career there in April 1965 and was cut up in February 1966. (D.K.Jones)

62) Leaving several more viaducts behind us, the next port of call is Liskeard, the starting point for trains travelling to Looe and Caradon. On 13th July 1955 smoke issues from the funnel of GWR 4500 Class 2-6-2T No 4568 (83E St.Blazey) as it rests with the stock of a passenger train from Looe in Liskeard station. Towards the end of its working life, No 4568 was allocated to 83A Newton Abbot and 83G Penzance. It was withdrawn from the latter in February 1959. (F.Hornby)

63) Liskeard looking east on 18th August 1959. Approaching the camera with a mixed bag of vehicles is GWR 5700 Class 0-6-0PT No 4679, from 83D Laira (Plymouth), which is in charge of a down pick-up freight. A long-term resident of Laira, No 4679 parted company with the depot in April 1962 moving to 86A Newport (Ebbw Junction). It remained in South Wales until condemnation in May 1965 after serving from the sheds at 88E Abercynon and 88B Cardiff (Radyr). (Peter Hay)

64) The West Country was savagely hit by the Beeching cuts in the sixties and one of the few branch lines still with us today is the one to Looe, ever popular with the bucket and spade brigade. On a sun-filled 12th April 1958 the platform is crowded with schoolchildren, one of which appears to be giving a 'Hitler salute' towards the camera. Simmering near to them is GWR 4500 Class 2-6-2T No 4565 (83E St.Blazey) which was taken out of service in October 1961. (R.S.Carpenter)

65) An immaculate twin set of non-corridor coaches are parked in front of the goods shed at Bodmin (General) on 9th June 1956. Attached to them bunker-first is another 83E St.Blazey locomotive in the shape of GWR 4500 Class 2-6-2T No 4569. Rendered redundant at St.Blazey shed in July 1961, No 4569 found a new home in West Wales at 87H Neyland. Later transfers between April 1963 and withdrawal in July 1964 took it to 82D Westbury, 83E Yeovil and 82C Swindon. (R.S.Carpenter)

66) Unlike Bodmin (General), closed in 1967, Bodmin Road is still operational today. Looking in pristine condition, 83G Penzance based GWR *Grange* Class 4-6-0 No 6826 *Nannerth Grange* disturbs the rural tranquility as it pauses in the station with an up 'stopper' on 8th September 1951. No 6826 remained faithful to Penzance shed until ousted by diesel power in July 1962. Withdrawn in May 1965 from 88A Cardiff East Dock it was scrapped at a yard in Swansea. (T.B.Owen)

67) 83E St.Blazey, a small enclosed half-roundhouse opened in 1872 and situated on the west side of a goods line between Par Harbour and the junction with the Par-Luxulyan line near St.Blazey station (closed in 1925), only ever had a small steam allocation most of which was involved in the movement of local china clay traffic. In steam alongside the depot building on 27th June 1950 is GWR 2021 Class 0-6-0PT No 2050 which was condemned later in the fifties. (R.S.Carpenter)

68) Another Cornish branch line which survived the Beeching Axe is the one from Par to Newquay, albeit with diesel traction. Back in the heady days of steam, GWR 4500 Class 2-6-2T No 5562 (83F Truro) is bathed in bright summer sunshine as it sets off from Newquay with the 10.50am local passenger bound for Falmouth on 16th August 1959. Withdrawn from 83G Penzance in September 1962, No 5562 was stored at the shed for over twelve months before being scrapped. (Peter Hay)

69) We return to the main line and find ourselves at St.Austell, where, on 1st September 1951, begrimed GWR *Manor* Class 4-6-0 No 7806 *Cockington Manor* pilots BR *Britannia* Class 4-6-2 No 70019 *Lightning* with a heavy express. Although only three months old when this photograph was taken, *Lightning* was destined for less than fifteen years of service and despite being condemned in March 1966 from 12A Carlisle (Kingmoor), No 70019 was not cut up until August 1967. (D.K.Jones)

70) One of the few centres of population in Cornwall is at Truro, famous for its splendid 19th Century cathedral. On a soaking wet 29th September 1958 a lone railwayman ignores the adverse conditions as he crosses the track in front of GWR *Castle* Class 4-6-0 No 4095 *Harlech Castle* which is in charge of the up *Cornish Riviera* express bound for Paddington. No 4095 had been an 83G Penzance steed since December 1957 following a transfer from 87E Landore (Swansea). (R.S.Carpenter)

71) Within the five short miles from Truro to Chacewater there are no less than three viaducts and a tunnel such is the nature of the terrain in deepest Cornwall. Under leaden skies, GWR *Grange* Class 4-6-0 No 6828 *Trellech Grange*, of 83F Truro, leaves Chacewater platform behind as it trundles onto Blackwater viaduct with an up stopping train on 15th August 1959. *Trellech Grange* took its leave of Truro shed in September 1961, moving to 84B Oxley. (Peter Hay)

72) The link between Chacewater and Newquay was broken during 1963 resulting with the closure of the intermediate stations at Mount Hawke Halt, St.Agnes, Goonbell Halt, Mithian Halt, Perranporth Beach Halt, Perranporth, Goonhavern Halt, Shepherds, Mitchell & Newlyn Halt and Trewerry & Trerice Halt. Pictured arriving at Shepherds station shortly before withdrawal is GWR 4500 Class 2-6-2T No 5500 (83F Truro) which is in charge of a local in August 1959. (Peter Hay)

73) Under clear signals, GWR *Hall* Class 4-6-0 No 5969 *Honington Hall*, allocation not known, arrives at St.Erth with a down local passenger train in August 1955. Note the St.Ives branch train in the left of the frame which has a GWR 4500 Class 2-6-2T as its motive power. Records show us that *Honington Hall* was later allocated to 81F Oxford, 82B St.Philip's Marsh, 87J Goodwick and 87G Carmarthen prior to withdrawal from the latter during August 1962. (R.S.Carpenter)

74) Representatives of the Hawksworth GWR *County* Class 4-6-0's were a common sight in the West Country with examples being shedded at 83D Laira, 83F Truro and 83G Penzance. Truro based No 1023 *County of Oxford* passes the diminutive signalbox at St.Erth on 8th July 1955 with a Penzance bound express. Modified with a double chimney in May 1957, No 1023 also worked from 83C Exeter St.Davids, 82C Swindon and 89A Shrewsbury before being condemned in March 1963. (R.W.Hinton)

75) The four-road straight running shed and repair shop at Penzance was opened in 1914 replacing a smaller structure which was adjacent to the station. The new depot then became a twenty-five minute walk from this Cornish terminus. Once diesel traction was introduced into the area it was not long before the former inmates were ousted (September 1962). In steam outside the shed on 8th July 1956 is resident GWR *Grange* Class 4-6-0 No 6824 *Ashley Grange*. (R.S.Carpenter)

76) Another long-term resident at 83G was GWR *Grange* Class 4-6-0 No 6808 *Beenham Grange* which is noted fully coaled between the turntable and the running shed in 1960. Upon closure to steam, *Beenham Grange* was transferred to 88L Cardiff East Dock. During the occasion of the author's only visit to this shed on 29th April 1962 there were fourteen steam engines present which included one GWR *County* Class 4-6-0 No 1001 *County of Bucks* and several *Granges*. (R.S.Carpenter)

77) 83D Laira (Plymouth) based GWR *Modified Hall* Class 4-6-0 No 6988 *Swithland Hall* has a clear path as it commences its journey to Plymouth shortly after departing from Penzance with an up express on 25th August 1956. *Swithland Hall* served at 82A Bristol (Bath Road) from September 1959 to September 1960 before returning to Laira for a final spell until September 1963. Its last haunt was at 82D Westbury, being withdrawn from there in September 1964. (N.L.Browne)

78) We finish our westward journey to Penzance with this shot of GWR *Grange* Class 4-6-0 No 6816 *Frankton Grange*, another Laira steed, which is noted backing empty stock consisting of four carriages and two vans out of the terminus on a dull 25th August 1956. Constructed at Swindon Works by December 1936, No 6816 also worked from the local shed at 83G and at 82B St.Philip's Marsh, 82E Bristol Barrow Road and 85A Worcester before being condemned in July 1965. (N.L.Browne)

79) Our westward journey on Southern Region metals commences in the cathedral city of Salisbury where on a damp and miserable 30th August 1951 SR Unrebuilt *Merchant Navy* Class 4-6-2 No 35023 *Holland-Afrika Line* is in charge of a passenger train. Built in November 1948, *Holland-Afrika Line* was rebuilt at Eastleigh Works in February 1957. During the latter years of its life it was based at the depots at Exmouth Junction, Bournemouth, Weymouth and Nine Elms. (B.K.B.Green)

80) Another SR Unrebuilt *Merchant Navy* Class 4-6-2 is captured by the camera at Salisbury station on 9th May 1952. With a clear road ahead December 1944 constructed (also rebuilt in February 1957) No 35012 *United States Lines* readies itself for departure with an express. *United States Lines* spent much of its working life allocated to 70A Nine Elms. After a spell at 70G Weymouth, from September 1964 until March 1967, it returned for a final stint at Nine Elms. (D.K.Jones)

81) In steam days it was not uncommon for Western Region locomotives to put in appearances at Salisbury station and from 1899 until complete closure in November 1950 the WR had its own standard gauge depot. On a sun-filled 27th June 1956, GWR *Hall* Class 4-6-0 No 4982 *Acton Hall*, from 86A Newport (Ebbw Junction) and paired with a straight-sided tender, heads an express. Withdrawn from 83D Laira (Plymouth) in May 1962, No 4982 was scrapped at Swindon. (D.K.Jones)

82) Like all of the regions the Southern had its fair share of BR standard locomotives and Class 5 4-6-0 No 73043 arrived at 71A Eastleigh in December 1962 by way of 10C Patricroft (LMR), 41B Grimesthorpe and 41D Canklow (ER). It is noted light engine at Salisbury on 27th July 1963. Later in its career it was based at 70B Feltham, Eastleigh (again), 70C Guildford and 70A Nine Elms. Although withdrawn in July 1967, No 73043 was not cut up until September 1968. (B.W.L.Brooksbank)

83) The Maunsell designed (1928) SR U Class 2-6-0's had a power classification of 4P3F and numbered a total of fifty units, including some examples rebuilt from the K Class 'River' 2-6-4 Tanks originally built in 1917. On 12th October 1961, No 31631 arrives at Salisbury with coaching stock. A longstanding resident of 70C Guildford, No 31631 was condemned from there in September 1963 and after a brief period of storage was scrapped at Eastleigh Works. (D.K.Jones)

84) With a member of the footplate crew looking towards the camera, SR S15 Class 4-6-0 No 30823, based locally at 72B, steams towards the camera with a passenger train at Salisbury in 1960. These versatile engines (6F) were of the mixed traffic variety and were employed in many parts of the Southern system. Of the forty-five units built seven are either preserved or awaiting restoration today, these being Nos 30499, 30506, 30825, 30828, 30830, 30841 and 30847. (D.K.Jones)

85) The spacious and airy MPD at Salisbury, coded 72B and 70E under BR, had, from January 1957 until April 1967, a number of BR Class 4 2-6-0's on its books (though not all at the same time) these being Nos 76005-9/17-19/53-55/59/60/66/67. In September 1961, No 76007 simmers gently in the shed yard. Drafted to 70F Bournemouth in April 1967, No 76007 survived until the end of steam on the Southern in July of the same year and was scrapped at Birds, Risca. (N.E.Preedy)

86) Designed in the latter part of the last Century the SR G6 Class 0-6-0 Tanks were down to a total of ten units by January 1957, two of which, Nos 30266 and 30270 were allocated to Salisbury shed. On 26th May 1957, No 30266 rests in the shed yard between shunting duties. Of the two, No 30270 was withdrawn in January 1959. No 30266 followed suit in June 1960 and both were scrapped at Eastleigh Works. Salisbury depot closed to steam in July 1967. (D.K.Jones)

87) We take our leave of Salisbury and head westwards on the SR main line from Waterloo to Exeter. On 16th September 1963, SR Rebuilt *West Country* Class 4-6-2 No 34101 *Hartland*, from 70A Nine Elms, bursts from beneath a road bridge near to Sherborne with a down express. Once of the Central Division and allocated to 73A Stewarts Lane and 73B Bricklayers Arms, *Hartland* was withdrawn from Eastleigh shed in July 1966. Today, it is preserved at the Peak Railway. (N.E.Preedy)

88) The sun beats down upon the railway scene near Yeovil Junction on 17th August 1963. SR Unrebuilt *Battle of Britain* Class 4-6-2 No 34075 *264 Squadron*, of 72A Exmouth Junction, heads homewards at speed with a down express from Waterloo. Transferred to Exmouth Junction in September 1957 from 74B Ramsgate, *264 Squadron* was not as fortunate as *Hartland*. After condemnation in April 1964 it was stored for a while before being despatched to Birds, Bridgend. (N.E.Preedy)

89) SR Unrebuilt *Battle of Britain* Class 4-6-2 No 34049 *Anti-Aircraft Command* (72B Salisbury) leaves a trail of black exhaust as it nears Yeovil Junction with another Waterloo to West of England express during high summer on 25th July 1963. Constructed in December 1946, *Anti-Aircraft Command* was one of the first examples of the class to be taken out of service, in November 1963. Stored unwanted at Eastleigh until May 1964 it was scrapped at the nearby works. (N.E.Preedy)

90) We complete this pictorial quartet of Bulleid Pacifics with this shot of SR Rebuilt *Merchant Navy* Class 4-6-2 No 35020 *Bibby Line*, from 70A Nine Elms, as it steams towards Yeovil Junction with a down express on 23rd July 1963. This was the last full year of express steam haulage on the Waterloo to Exeter route. *Bibby Line*, constructed in June 1945 and rebuilt in April 1956, was taken out of traffic in February 1965 and cut up the following month. (N.E.Preedy)

91) The demise of the former Great Western Railway shed at Yeovil Pen Mill in January 1959, situated between the junction of lines from Pen Mill station, Weymouth and Yeovil Town, brought many ex. GWR types to the SR depot adjacent to the Town station where they intermixed with SR locomotives. Before the closure of Pen Mill shed (82E/71H), GWR 5700 Class 0-6-0PT No 8745, light engine, poses for the camera at Yeovil in bright sunshine on 7th September 1957. (B.K.B.Green)

92) Despite the mass introduction of diesel multiple units on suburban services over most of the BR system some areas of the Southern Region remained unscathed and still operated steam powered push and pull trains as late as 1963. On 22nd August of the same year, GWR 5400 Class 0-6-0PT No 5410 rests between such duties at Yeovil Town station whilst awaiting its next short journey to Yeovil Junction. No 5410, however, was withdrawn two months later. (D.K.Jones)

93) The 'humble' rubs shoulders with the 'mighty' in the yard at 72C Yeovil on a drab-looking 19th March 1963. In the frame is resident GWR 4500 Class 2-6-2T No 4507, which, in common with No 5410 in the previous picture was also withdrawn in October 1963. To the left of No 4507 is SR Unrebuilt *West Country* Class 4-6-2 No 34023 *Blackmore Vale*, from 72A Exmouth Junction. No 4507, the last engine built at Wolverhampton Works, was cut up at Birds, Risca in June 1964. (D.K.Jones)

94) On 23rd March 1963, GWR 6100 Class 2-6-2T No 6113, a visitor from 83B Taunton, has been seconded by the depot hierarchy at Yeovil to perform on shed pilot duties. Later in the year, November, No 6113 was drafted to pastures new in South Wales at 88B Cardiff (Radyr). A final move in November 1964 took it to 85B Gloucester (Horton Road). Yeovil shed closed completely in June 1965 and its last remaining steam stock was transferred to other depots. (D.K.Jones)

95) Having left Yeovil behind along with the stations at Sutton Bingham (closed in 1962), Crewkerne and Chard Junction (closed in 1966), we halt briefly at Axminster which displays a small goods depot along with a variety of upper quadrant, dummy and repeater signals. Completing the picture is SR S15 Class 4-6-0, No 30845 (72A Exmouth Junction), which is struggling for adhesion as it approaches the station with a heavy freight on 30th August 1951. (B.K.B.Green)

96) It is impossible to progress westwards without a visit to the famous Lyme Regis branch which for so many years was the haunt of the trio of 72A Exmouth Junction based Adams SR 0415 Class 4-4-2 Tanks until displaced by diesel multiple units in July 1961. Despite being in the latter stages of its lengthy working life, No 30583 looks a sight for sore eyes as it gently lifts its safety valves at Axminster station with the branch train in the summer of 1960. (B.K.B.Green)

97) This photograph epitomizes the once timeless branch line scene on British Railways when steam was king. A smattering of folk and the 'family dog' pause momentarily as the photographer's shutter is clicked, mainly to record the presence of SR 0415 Class 4-4-2T No 30582 which sizzles in the platform at Lyme Regis on 29th August 1955. Seventy-one of these engines were built between 1882 and 1885 and all but three (BR Nos 30582-84) were scrapped in the 1920's. (N.L.Browne)

98) A handful of enthusiasts mill around the platform at Lyme Regis on a damp 28th June 1953 which was the occasion of a special organised by the Stephenson Locomotive Society. The special is being hauled jointly by SR 0415 Class 4-4-2T No 30583 and SR Terrier A1X Class 0-6-0T No 32662. Who would have guessed in those far-off days that both engines would end up being preserved - No 30583 at the Bluebell Railway and No 32662 at Bressingham. (B.K.B.Green)

99) Unlike Nos 30583 and 32662 in the previous picture, BR Class 9F 2-10-0 No 92220 *Evening Star* was destined for preservation as soon as it was released into traffic in March 1960 for having the dubious distinction of being the last steam locomotive to be built for BR. On 28th September 1964 *Evening Star* (88A Cardiff East Dock) is in charge of a 'Farewell To Steam' railtour at Seaton Junction. By this date this area was firmly in the grip of the WR authorities (D.Webster)

100) More special traffic, this time at Colyton station on the Seaton branch on 26th February 1965. Specially spruced-up by the shed staff at 83D Exmouth Junction, BR Class 4 2-6-4T No 80041 powers the 'East Devon Tour'. Upon the closure of Exmouth Junction depot in June 1965, No 80041 was transferred to 83G Templecombe where it eked out its last days on the former Somerset & Dorset lines. Withdrawn in March 1966 it was cut up four months later. (D.Webster)

101) Up until the early sixties 72A Exmouth Junction had the sub-sheds at Bude, Callington, Exmouth, Lyme Regis, Okehampton and Seaton under its wing. Pictured outside the single line structure at the latter on 9th September 1960 is 72A based SR M7 Class 0-4-4T No 30045. These small depots closed one by one either as diesels encroached on the scene or the various branch lines were closed under the Beeching Axe. The link to Seaton closed to passengers in 1966. (B.K.B.Green)

102) Moving back to the main line briefly we find ourselves at Honiton, where, on 17th June 1963, a rather less-than-clean SR Unrebuilt *Battle of Britain* Class 4-6-2 No 34078 *222 Squadron*, a 72A Exmouth Junction mount, has paused at the station with the 8.55am Ilfracombe to Salisbury express. In common with the majority of Bulleid Pacifics allocated to Exmouth Junction, *222 Squadron* was condemned in September 1964. It was scrapped three months later. (J.D.Gomersall)

103) The following three prints are once again devoted to branch lines in Devon, the first being at Tipton St.Johns (closed in 1967), the junction for Sidmouth and Exmouth. LMS Class 2 2-6-2T No 41206 (83D Exmouth Junction), once of 24H Hellifield, 26E Lees, 27A Bank Hall and 83H Plymouth (Friary), is paired with GWR 5700 Class 0-6-0PT No 4666 (also of Exmouth Junction shed) as part of the LCGB inspired 'East Devon Tour' on 26th February 1965. (D.Webster)

104) A close-up of the second engine involved with No 41206 on 26th February 1965. GWR 5700 Class 0-6-0PT No 4666 looks in fine fettle as it lets off steam in Sidmouth station (closed in 1966). No 4666 had been transferred to The Southern Region as early as November 1959 from 87C Danygraig. Apart from its involvement at Exmouth Junction depot it was also shedded at 72F Wadebridge and 72E Barnstaple. No 4666 was condemned from Exmouth Junction four months later. (D.Webster)

105) Shrouded in bright sunshine, SR 02 Class 0-4-4T No 30232, yet another inmate of 72A Exmouth Junction, is captured on camera out of steam in the yard of the diminutive sub-shed at Exmouth on 9th July 1956. Designed between 1889 and 1923 by Adams with some modifications by Drummond, the class had been reduced to only thirty-seven working examples by January 1957. The mainland members were withdrawn by December 1962, with No 30232 having gone in September 1959. (R.W.Hinton)

106) The next four prints depict the work of a photographer who recorded Southern steam in its eleventh hour on the Waterloo to Exeter main line at Pinhoe on the outskirts of Exeter on 28th August 1964. The fireman of begrimed SR Rebuilt *West Country* Class 4-6-2 No 34032 *Camelford* (70E Salisbury) takes things easy as his charge heads towards Exeter with a down train. Built in June 1946 and rebuilt in October 1960, No 34032 was withdrawn in October 1966. (Alan Jones)

107) The sun beats down and summer foliage abounds near to one of the platforms at Pinhoe as SR Unrebuilt *West Country* Class 4-6-2 No 34030 *Watersmeet* (83D Exmouth Junction) speeds towards the camera bound for Exeter and beyond with a down express. *Watersmeet*, a long-term inhabitant of Exmouth Junction shed bowed to the inevitable in light of advancing modernisation in September 1964. After a brief period of storage at 83D it was scrapped by Birds, Morriston. (Alan Jones)

108) The final member of the thirty strong SR Rebuilt *Merchant Navy* Class 4-6-2's, No 35030 *Elder Dempster Lines*, from 70A Nine Elms, accelerates through Pinhoe with a Waterloo bound express. Constructed under the ownership of British Railways in April 1949, *Elder Dempster Lines* was rebuilt in April 1958. A longstanding inmate of Nine Elms it was drafted to 70G Weymouth a month after this picture was taken. It was cut up in South Wales in November 1968. (Alan Jones)

109) The final photograph in this sequence shows the fine lines of SR Rebuilt *Battle of Britain* Class 4-6-2 No 34059 *Sir Archibald Sinclair*, of 70E Salisbury, motionless in Pinhoe station with an up stopping train. Condemned from Salisbury in May 1966, six years after being rebuilt, No 34059 languished in store at Eastleigh shed for a while before being despatched to Barry Docks. It was rescued by the Bluebell Railway in October 1979. (Alan Jones)

110) Exmouth Junction shed with its host of interior tracks was a mecca for steam enthusiasts and on 21st June 1964 the locomotives present in the shed yard belies the fact that the majority would be withdrawn within the next three months. From left to right are SR N Class 2-6-0 No 31855, BR Class 5 4-6-0 No 73155, LMR Class 2 2-6-2 Tanks Nos 41206 and 41295 and SR Unrebuilt *West Country* and *Battle of Britain* Class 4-6-2's Nos 34063/57/33/81/20. (P.B.Hands)

111) Exmouth Junction depot had a legion of the SR N Class 2-6-0's on its books, many of which were utilised on former London & South Western metals to the west of Exeter. Parked in bright sunshine in the yard at 72A, with no visible identification markings, is No 31853, on 17th April 1949. Taken out of revenue earning service at Exmouth Junction in September 1964, No 31853 was initially stored at 83C Exeter St.Davids prior to scrapping later in the year. (B.K.B.Green)

112) The SR U Class 2-6-0's were another variation of this wheel arrangement to be housed at Exmouth Junction, though not in as many numbers as the N Class. On 28th July 1949, No 31634, with the lettering of its relatively new owner stencilled on the tender, awaits its next rostered duty next to SR Unrebuilt *West Country* Class 4-6-2 No 34016 *Bodmin*. No 31634, withdrawn from 70A Nine Elms in December 1963, was scrapped at Eastleigh Works in February 1964. (R.W.Hinton)

113) The LSWR 0395 Class 0-6-0's, designed by Adams, were constructed between 1881 and 1886 and all in all a total of seventy were built. Many examples of them were shipped to Palestine and Mesopotamia during the Great War. One of their ranks, No 30581, clearly showing the spartan protection from the cab for the footplate crew, is dead in the yard at 72A on 1st September 1952. The class became extinct with the withdrawal of No 30567 in September 1959. (D.K.Jones)

114) SR Rebuilt *Battle of Britain* Class 4-6-2 No 34088 *213 Squadron*, from 70A Nine Elms, is in shocking external condition, as, fully coaled, it steams through Exeter Central station to take up a passenger duty on 2nd August 1964. Once of 73A Stewarts Lane, No 34088 had been ousted from the Central Division in May 1961 moving initially to Nine Elms and then to 75A Brighton before returning for another spell at 70A in July 1963. It died in March 1967. (D.Webster)

115) With a diesel multiple unit lurking in the right background, one of the ubiquitous SR N Class 2-6-0's No 31859, also in a filthy condition, nears the end of its working life at the head of a local passenger at Exeter Central on 28th August 1964. No 31859 found its way to 72A in August 1963 by way of 73C Hither Green, 75C Norwood Junction, 75A Brighton and 70C Guildford. Three months after withdrawal in September 1964 it was cut up in South Wales. (Alan Jones)

116) Apart from the absence of steam locomotives Exeter Central is much the same today as it was in the sixties. In the right of the picture are a variety of goods wagons in the sidings as, in the left of the frame, LMS Ivatt Class 2 2-6-2T No 41308, locally based at Exmouth Junction, tracks through the station light engine on 28th August 1964. No 41308, once of 73E Faversham and 73F Ashford, survived the mass withdrawals from 83D in September 1964. (Alan Jones)

117) Sunlight and shadow at Exeter Central station in June 1955. The nearest platform to us throngs with passengers as 72D Plymouth (Friary) allocated SR Unrebuilt *West Country* Class 4-6-2 No 34036 *Westward Ho* takes a breather after arriving with an express. From November 1957 until withdrawal in July 1967, *Westward Ho* was subjected to a number of transfers - 72A Exmouth Junction (11/57), 70E Salisbury (10/63), 70D Eastleigh (9/64) and 70A Nine Elms (6/66). (D.K.Jones)

118) Barnstaple Junction and nearby locoshed was the property of the Southern Region of BR until December 1962 when the WR took control. Approaching the station bunker-first on 19th May 1956 is locally based (72E) LMS Class 2 2-6-2T No 41298 which is hauling the 12.18pm local from Torrington. The tracks veering off to the right lead to Barnstaple Town and Ilfracombe. No 41298 took its leave of Barnstaple shed in March 1963, moving to 71A Eastleigh. (N.E.Preedy)

119) Freight traffic in the Barnstaple area was sparce at the best of times and it was perhaps unusual to see one hauled by a Bulleid light Pacific. On a summer's day in 1963 SR Unrebuilt *West Country* Class 4-6-2 No 34106 *Lydford*, from 72A Exmouth Junction, readies itself for a journey to Exeter. In common with sister engines Nos 34020, 34030, 34054, 34078, 34080, 34096, 34107 and 34109, *Lynton* was withdrawn from Exmouth Junction in September 1964. (Peter Hands)

120) Two members of the depot staff at Barnstaple Junction peer towards the photographer from the entrance to the running shed on 27th June 1953. The main focus of attention is on a rather less than clean SR T9 'Greyhound' Class 4-4-0 No 30708 in steam in the yard paired with its distinctive, but rather ungainly-looking eight-wheeled tender. A 72A Exmouth Junction steed, No 30708 was condemned in December 1957 almost seven years before Barnstaple shed closed. (F.Hornby)

121) Ilfracombe possessed a neat and tidy terminus station (closed in 1970) along with some carriage sidings and a compact, but small depot (a sub-shed to Barnstaple Junction). Posing in the rain is yet another 72A Exmouth Junction locomotive, SR N Class 2-6-0 No 31832 which is in charge of a local passenger on 17th April 1954. Along with sister engines, Nos 31830/31/33, No 31832 took its leave of 72A in August 1962, moving to 75A Brighton. (B.K.B.Green)

122) Thanks to Doctor Beeching the former London & South Western Railway branches in North Devon, west of Barnstaple, were decimated in the mid-sixties and the next eight prints have the years of closure of the stations photographed in brackets. With smart dwellings providing a backdrop, SR M7 Class 0-4-4T No 30247 (72E Barnstaple Junction) steams into Instow (1965) with the 4.28pm local from Barnstaple to Torrington. No 30247 was withdrawn in October 1961. (N.E.Preedy)

123) Considering its remoteness, Torrington (1965) had a reasonably sized railway layout. Letting off steam nearest the camera is LMS Class 2 2-6-2T No 41298, another inhabitant of Barnstaple Junction shed, with a single-coach train bound for Halwill Junction in 1961. Fussing about in the background with some goods wagons is an unidentified sister engine. Later in its career, No 41298 also served from the sheds at 70G Weymouth and 70A Nine Elms. (D.K.Jones)

66

124) It is not hard to realise why the branch lines in North Devon were under threat when all we see in this picture are three
BR members of staff at Hatherleigh station (1965) on a gloomy 9th May 1963. As the fireman rakes out some ash, his charge,
LMS Class 2 2-6-2T No 41216 (72E) takes refreshment from one of the station's water columns. No 41216, once of 6K Rhyl
and 83H Plymouth (Friary), is in charge of the 4.00pm local from Torrington to Halwill. (J.Schatz)

125) We reach Halwill Junction (1966) the crossroads for the lines to and from Barnstaple, Bude, Launceston, Bow and Bere
Alston. In the left of the frame on an overcast day in May 1961 is 72A Exmouth Junction allocated SR Unrebuilt *West
Country* Class 4-6-2 No 34033 *Chard* and in the right of the frame is an unidentified LMS Class 2 2-6-2T with a branch train.
Ousted from Exmouth Junction shed in September 1964, *Chard* found a new home at 70D Eastleigh. (N.E.Preedy)

126) A panoramic view of Halwill Junction station with its fine array of upper quadrant signals and lofty signalbox on 6th May 1963. Two members of the railway fraternity watch the arrival of SR N Class 2-6-0 No 31843, from 72A Exmouth Junction and in filthy external condition, which is heading the two-coach 12.58pm passenger from Padstow to Okehampton. A longstanding inmate of Exmouth Junction shed, No 31843 was withdrawn in September 1964. (J.Schatz)

127) Holsworthy station (1966), between Halwill Junction and Bude, is the setting for this next print. The external condition and allocation of SR N Class 2-6-0 No 31846 is a replica of the previous photograph. Suitcases, boxes and suitcases abound on the opposite platform as No 31846 prepares for departure with the 1.18pm from Okehampton to Bude on 6th May 1963. Another victim of the September 1964 withdrawals, No 31846 was scrapped three months later. (J.Schatz)

128) The next two photographs depict the 'Old Order' on former LSWR metals. The first is of the now long-gone terminus station at Bude (1966). Occupying the station on a sun-drenched 22nd May 1956 are some cattle trucks, a parcels van, a single van and SR T9 'Greyhound' Class 4-4-0 No 30717 (72A Exmouth Junction) which is powering a train consisting of two carriages and a van. Taken out of revenue earning traffic in July 1961, No 30717 was cut up at Eastleigh Works. (N.E.Preedy)

129) The second photograph from 'memory lane' takes us to Okehampton (1972 except for excursion traffic). A member of the footplate crew of SR T9 Class 4-4-0 No 30729, also from 72A and in pristine external condition, poses for the camera as it heads a train tender-first on 17th April 1954. No 30729 later served from the sheds at 70F Fratton and 72B Salisbury before returning for a final stint at 72A in May 1960. It was condemned from there in March 1961. (B.K.B.Green)

130) We leave the branch lines of North Devon behind and arrive in Plymouth, where, up until complete closure on 5th May 1963, the Southern Region had a small three-road MPD at Friary, coded 72D and 83H under BR. For the spotter on foot this was a difficult shed to locate, being approximately three-quarters of a mile from Friary station (closed in 1958). In steam on a gloomy 3rd October 1949 is SR Unrebuilt *West Country* Class 4-6-2 No 34011 *Tavistock*. (R.S.Carpenter)

131) With most potential travellers sheltering out of sight from the pouring rain at Plymouth (North Road), SR Unrebuilt *West Country* Class 4-6-2 No 34023 *Blackmore Vale*, of 72A Exmouth Junction, awaits departure with the 4.52pm passenger train to Waterloo via Eastleigh on 19th June 1963. This train was timed to arrive at Waterloo in the early hours of the following day! Withdrawn from 70A Nine Elms in July 1967, No 34023 is preserved at the Bluebell Railway. (J.D.Gomersall)

132) We continue our meandering journey and make our way inland again to Tavistock which once boasted two stations on two different routes, South (GWR), closed in 1962 and North (SR), closed in 1968. On a dull 17th August 1958, SR Unrebuilt *Battle of Britain* Class 4-6-2 No 34081 *92 Squadron*, from 72A Exmouth Junction (surprise, surprise!) enters Tavistock North with a Waterloo to Plymouth express. Withdrawal for No 34081 came in August 1964. (R.S.Carpenter)

133) We venture up the Callington branch, where, in contrasts of bright sunshine and deep shadow, begrimed 83H Plymouth (Friary) LMS Class 2 2-6-2T No 41316 lurks in the platform at the small terminus with a local passenger in 1960. This station, of Plymouth, Devonport and South Western Railway origin, closed during 1966. Before its demise in October 1966, No 41316 went on to work from the sheds at Laira, Exmouth Junction, Nine Elms and Bournemouth. (Peter Hay)

134) Like many branch line termini, Callington possessed its own small sub-shed. This is a fine picture of the depot, where LMS Class 2 2-6-2T No 41206, another Plymouth (Friary) inhabitant, shares the tracks with a coal wagon on 15th April 1962. This depot closed in situ on 1st September 1964. No 41206 moved on to 72A Exmouth Junction in February 1963 and when the latter closed in June 1965 it was drafted to a final home at 83G Templecombe, being withdrawn in March 1966. (N.E.Preedy)

135) The westernmost motive power depot on the Southern Region was at Wadebridge in Cornwall, coded 72F and 84E in BR days. Out of steam and parked in the company of a SR 4-6-0 type in a siding at the shed in 1957 is SR 02 Class 0-4-4T No 30236, local to Wadebridge, which was condemned in January 1960 and scrapped at Eastleigh Works the following month. The shed closed in November 1964, its last inhabitants being GWR 1366 Class 0-6-0 Panniers, Nos 1367-1369. (R.S.Carpenter)

136) A busy scene at Wadebridge station on a dull 3rd September 1957, where, unlike in the previous photograph, No 30236 is seen in steam and is about to depart with a two-coach local passenger. To the right of the impressive signal gantry is SR T9 'Greyhound' Class 4-4-0 No 30710 (72A Exmouth Junction) on another passenger working. In the right of the frame we can just make out part of the two-road locoshed with the crude 'coaling facility' in the foreground. (Peter Hay)

137) Although of little importance in the overall scheme of British Railways, Wadebridge was unique in having the three surviving Beattie SR 0298 Class 2-4-0 Well Tanks based at the local shed and enthusiasts used to flock from far and wide to see them, especially in their latter years. This is a fine close-up of No 30586 on shunting duties in the vicinity of the goods shed in April 1958. In the right of the frame is SR N Class 2-6-0 No 31847, from 72A. (Peter Hay)

138) The driver and fireman are on the running plate of locally based SR O2 Class 0-4-4T No 30200 as they attend to a minor problem with their charge before departing to Bodmin on a sunny 4th May 1959. No 30200 was drafted away from 72F to 71A Eastleigh in March 1961. In the left background is SR 0298 Class 2-4-0WT No 30586 again. Of Nos 30585-87, this was the only one to be scrapped, at Eastleigh Works in March 1964, fifteen months after withdrawal. (R.S.Carpenter)

139) The main reason for the lengthy survival of the SR 0298 Class 2-4-0 Well Tanks was their use on the china clay trains on the tightly curved Wenford Bridge branch (until replaced by the GWR 1366 Class 0-6-0 Pannier Tanks during 1962). On 3rd September 1957, No 30587 is employed on such a duty. Withdrawn *en masse* from Wadebridge shed in December 1962 all three spent some considerable time stored at various locations. Today, Nos 30585/87 are preserved. (Peter Hay)

140) We reach the end of the line for the Southern Region in the West of England at the remote seaside resort of Padstow on the Atlantic Coast where the station and line from Wadebridge closed in 1967 leaving nothing but memories for those associated with the same. In happier times, on 3rd September 1957, SR T9 Class 'Greyhound' 4-4-0 No 30710 (72A Exmouth Junction) awaits departure from this small terminus. The loco survived in service until March 1959. (Peter Hay)

141) No photograph album covering the South West would be worth its salt without including the former Somerset & Dorset Joint Railway. This photograph is filled with nostalgia, with goods yards, goods vehicles, various signals and a signalbox on show at Bath Green Park. Completing the scene are locally based BR Class 5 4-6-0 No 73049 and an unidentified S & D Class 7F 2-8-0 which are departing for Bournemouth (West) with an express in August 1962. (N.E.Preedy)

142) An unusual tender-end view of S & D Class 7F 2-8-0 No 53809 recently outshopped with the second style of BR 'Lion on Wheel' emblem as seen in November 1961. The cylinder cocks are open as the locomotive makes a 'cold' start from Bath goods yard with a freight. Withdrawn from Green Park shed in June 1964, No 53809 was despatched to Barry Docks where it lay rotting and stripped of dignity until saved for posterity by the Midland Railway Centre in October 1970. (Peter Hay)

143) Another view of the lines around Bath Green Park station, this time on 20th February 1958. The skyline is dominated by two large gasometers and in the left of the picture is an impressive signal gantry and a loading gauge. The main feature is of a lengthy freight train departing with S & D Class 7F 2-8-0 No 53809 at its head. Bringing up the rear is LMS Class 4F 0-6-0 No 44558. Both locomotives, which have steam to spare, are shedded locally. On 23rd of this same month the WR took over the operation of the S & D. (T.R.Amos)

144) Green Park MPD consisted of two straight running sheds. The larger of the two was ex. S & D, whilst the smaller had once been the property of the Midland Railway. At the latter on 14th June 1960 spotters make their notes whilst on an official visit. On show in front of the shed are two LMS Class 4F 0-6-0's, Nos 44146 and 44523, both natives of the shed. During this same month, No 44523 was transferred to 82E Bristol Barrow road where it died in August 1963. (B.Wilson)

145) A sylvan setting in the North Somerset countryside near to Bath where the line curves and snakes into the distance. Nearing the camera is the final member of the former Midland Railway Class 2P 4-4-0's, No 40700 (82F Bath Green Park), which is powering a local passenger on 10th May 1958. These useful locomotives were a common sight on the S & D until replaced by more modern types. Condemned in September 1962, No 40700 was cut up at Derby Works. (D.K.Jones)

146) Midford must have been one of the most popular and picturesque settings on British Railways and the author makes no apologies for using the same location for the next three prints. Under blue skies punctuated by 'powder-puff clouds', BR Class 4 4-6-0 No 75009, of 82G Templecombe, pilots S & D Class 7F 2-8-0 No 53807, from 82F Bath Green Park and with safety valves blowing, with a heavy Bournemouth bound service from the Midlands in the summer of 1962. (N.E.Preedy)

147) The pioneer BR Class 9F 2-10-0 No 92000, constructed by January 1954 and equipped with a double chimney, sweeps majestically past the small platform at Midford and heads for Bournemouth with a holiday express in August 1961. Allocated to 86A Newport (Ebbw Junction) from new, No 92000 had been drafted to 82F Bath Green Park in June 1961. Five months later it was transferred away, but returned to Green Park shed for the summer service of 1962. (N.E.Preedy)

148) A little boy stands near the security of a fence at Midford as his father admires the passing of a Bournemouth bound express filled with excited holidaymakers in August 1962. Double-heading the train are BR Class 4 4-6-0 No 75023 (82G Templecombe) and SR Rebuilt *West Country* Class 4-6-2 No 34045 *Ottery St.Mary*, of 71B Bournemouth. Less than four years on and both engines were gone for ever, No 34045 in June 1964 followed by No 75023 in January 1966. (N.E.Preedy)

149) We journey on to Wellow, a few short miles from Midford, where, on 16th August 1965 a rather bedraggled-looking BR Class 5 4-6-0 No 73001, from Green Park shed and sporting a home-made front numberplate, momentarily disturbs the greenery of the embankments as it rounds a bend and approaches the camera in full cry whilst in charge of the 9.48am passenger from Bath to Bournemouth. No 73001 was withdrawn from service at 82F in December 1965. (T.R.Amos)

150) The most famed train to traverse the S & D was *The Pines* express from Manchester to Bournemouth via Birmingham (New Street) until it was re-routed via Birmingham (Snow Hill) and Oxford at the end of the 1962 summer service. On 22nd August 1959 *The Pines* is entrusted to LMS Class 4F 0-6-0 No 44424 (82E Bristol Barrow Road) and SR Unrebuilt *West Country* Class 4-6-2 No 34041 *Wilton* (71B Bournemouth) as they pass Shoscombe and Single Hill Halt. (B.W.L.Brooksbank)

151) In sharp contrast to the previous 'summer' photos it is deep winter at Radstock station on 24th December 1963 where there is a heavy coating of frost on the boards in the foreground. BR Class 5 4-6-0 No 73052 (82F Bath Green Park) is shrouded in leaking steam as it passes the north signalbox with a passenger train bound for Templecombe. Allocated to Green Park shed from new in June 1954, No 73052 was taken out of service from there in December 1964. (D.K.Jones)

152) Bath Green Park depot had two sub-sheds under its wing, at Highbridge East and Radstock. Based at the latter on a semi-permanent basis were the two members of the unique Geared Sentinel 0-4-0 Tanks Nos 47190 and 47191. These single-speed engines had been built for the S & D in 1929. On shed at Radstock on 4th June 1955 is No 47191 which was withdrawn in August 1959. It was scrapped at a yard in Wigan after a period of storage at Badnall Wharf. (D.K.Jones)

153) A feather of steam escapes from the safety valves of BR Class 4 2-6-0 No 76013, from 70F Bournemouth, as it disturbs the rustic tranquility of the countryside near to Chilcompton station with a passenger working on a warm 16th August 1965. No 76013 was a once longstanding resident of Eastleigh shed until drafted to Bournemouth in September 1964. Condemned in September 1966 it was stored at Eastleigh before being despatched for scrapping to a yard in South Wales. (T.R.Amos)

154) The fiercest gradient on the Somerset and Dorset was the one leading to Masbury summit and heavier trains had to be double-headed in most instances. On 14th September 1957, LMS Class 2P 4-4-0 No 40695 and BR Class 5 4-6-0 No 73047 round a curve near to the summit with the 4.30pm Bath to Bournemouth express. Both Nos 40696 and 73047 were allocated to Green Park shed, which at this stage in time belonged to the Southern Region, being coded 71G. (John Head)

155) Bright sunshine highlights the station buildings at Masbury as BR Class 4 4-6-0 No 75072, of Green Park shed , arrives with the 8.15am passenger from Bath to Templecombe on 12th September 1957. Constructed in November 1955, No 75072 was initially based at 72A Exmouth Junction. It was transferred to Green Park in June 1956 and remained there until October 1962 moving to a final abode at Templecombe. It acquired a double chimney in November 1960. (John Head)

156) BR Class 5 4-6-0 No 73001 (82F) pauses briefly at Shepton Mallet (Charlton Road) station to replenish its water supply whilst working the 9.00am Bristol to Bournemouth passenger on 16th October 1965. Introduced into service at 17A Derby in May 1951, No 73001 later worked from the sheds at 84G Shrewsbury, 82C Swindon, 82E Bristol Barrow Road and 85B Gloucester (Horton Road) before arriving at Green Park in February 1965. It was cut up in May 1966. (Ken Ellis)

157) Evercreech was the junction for the line to Glastonbury and Highbridge, the latter being the connection for trains on the Bristol to West of England main line. A member of the station staff at Evercreech turns his back on an unkempt-looking LMS Class 4F 0-6-0 No 44558 (82F) which is employed on the 4.35pm local from Bath to Templecombe on a dull 30th March 1964. No 44558 was one of a small batch of such engines constructed for the S & D in 1922. (J.Schatz)

158) 30th March 1964 seems to be the day of the 'dirty engine' at Evercreech Junction as can be witnessed by the disgraceful condition of SR Unrebuilt *West Country* Class 4-6-2 No 34041 *Wilton*, allocated to 70F Bournemouth. *Wilton* is in charge of the 3.35pm Bristol to Bournemouth passenger. Built in September 1946, No 34041 was a Bournemouth loco for many years. It losts its direct association with the depot in September 1964, moving to 70D Eastleigh. (J.Schatz)

159) Templecombe was the meeting point of the Somerset and Dorset and the Southern main line from Waterloo to Exeter. Nearing the end of its useful working life on 25th July 1963, LMS Class 4F 0-6-0 No 44411, from 82F Green Park (complete with single-line tablet catcher) is paired with an ancient carriage. Transferred to Green Park in May 1962 from 82E Bristol Barrow Road, No 44411 was condemned in October 1963 and was scrapped somewhat unusually at Swindon Works (N.E.Preedy)

160) Reflection time at Templecombe on 16th October 1965. Locally based at the nearby shed, LMS Class 2 2-6-2T No 41296 assists the 3.40pm Bournemouth to Bristol mail train up the bank into Templecombe (Upper). This locomotive chopped and changed its homes from January 1957 up until withdrawal in March 1966 -Barnstaple Junction, Highbridge, Templecombe, Bristol Barrow Road, Exmouth Junction and Templecombe again from September 1964 onwards. (Ken Ellis)

161) Cigarette dangling from his lips, a member of the footplate crew of LMS Class 2 2-6-2T No 41307 looks towards the camera as his charge trundles over some pointwork light engine at Templecombe on a bright and sunny 5th October 1965. For many years a regular at Exmouth Junction shed, No 41307 had moved on to Templecombe depot after the closure of the former in June 1965. Withdrawn in March 1966 it was cut up at Cohens, Morriston, Swansea four months later. (D.K.Jones)

162) Templecombe, coded 22D, 71H, 82G and 83G in BR days was situated between the lines to Bournemouth and the goods station. The original wooden shed was replaced by a brick-built structure in 1951. It only ever had a small number of engines on its books at any one time, including examples from the GWR, SR, LMS and BR standards. On 11th September 1960, two months before being drafted to 82E Bristol Barrow Road, LMS Class 2 2-6-2T No 41248 poses in the yard. (N.E.Preedy)

163) Back to back in the yard with No 41248 on the same day is LMS Class 2P 4-4-0 No 40569, another 83G inmate. The 2P's were popular locomotives on the S & D and were used in the main as pilots on double-headed trains until superseded by more modern steam engines in the early sixties. No 40569 survived in service at Templecombe shed until November 1961. After withdrawal it was stored at Crewe Works until summoned by the cutter's torch the following month. (N.E.Preedy)

164) Another popular breed of locomotives which graced S & D metals over the years was the LMS Class 4F 0-6-0's which were equally at home on passenger trains as well as freights. Parked out of steam near to the turntable at the rear of Templecombe shed in the late fifties is No 44102, for many years a favourite with the shed staff. It took its leave of 82G as a resident in October 1963, moving to Bath Green Park. It was condemned in September 1964. (R.Butterfield)

165) During its twilight years Templecombe shed acquired six BR Class 4 2-6-4 Tanks, Nos 80037, 80039, 80041, 80043, 80059 and 80067 (though not all at the same time). Of these, Nos 80037, 80041 and 80043 survived until the end on 7th March 1966. Several months earlier, two lads pose for the camera in front of No 80043 in the yard at 83G in bright sunlight on Saturday 16th October 1965. This depot and the one at Green Park were the last coded steam sheds on the WR. (Ken Ellis)

166) Tracking southwards we miss out Henstridge station and arrive at Stalbridge, where, after seeking the vantage point of the closed level crossing gates, the photographer photographed 82G Templecombe's LMS Class 2 2-6-2 No 41248 swathed in sunshine at the head of a local in the summer of 1959. Note the unusual second vehicle in the train formation. No 41248 had its relatively short career curtailed from 83F Barnstaple Junction in November 1964. (A.C.Ingram)

167) Another popular choice of steam traction over the main S & D route between Bath and Bournemouth were the BR Class 4 2-6-0's. Parcels are loaded onto a morning Bournemouth bound train at Blandford Forum station in 1960 as No 76015, from 71A Eastleigh, waits patiently for the off. Built in May 1953, No 76015 was transferred from Eastleigh to 71B Bournemouth in June 1961. Withdrawn from Bournemouth in October 1965 it was scrapped at Cohens, Morriston, Swansea. (A.C.Ingram)

168) Photographed from the carriage of an adjacent train, the fireman of GWR 5700 Class 0-6-0PT No 3758 stands atop his charge as it takes refreshment at Blandford Forum station whilst powering a local passenger on 13th July 1962. What this engine, allocated to 82C Swindon, was doing in this neck of the woods is somewhat of a mystery to the author. By coincidence it was allocated to 82F Bath Green Park in October 1964, being withdrawn from there in March 1966. (R.Picton)

169) After traversing Broadstone Junction the S & D merges with the former LSWR main line at Poole as we near our final destination at Bournemouth (West). The station is crowded with passengers as begrimed BR Class 4 2-6-0 No 76062 (71A Eastleigh) arrives with the 3.42pm from Bournemouth to Bristol on a gloomy 20th October 1962. Constructed in July 1955, No 76062 started its revenue earning service from 75B Redhill. It was condemned from Eastleigh in October 1965. (J.Schatz)

170) Branksome provided a depot to supply motive power from the southern end of the S & D, a sub-shed under the wing of Bournemouth. On the occasion of the author's only visit to the shed on a rain-lashed 21st January 1962 there were only two engines 'on shed', BR Class 5 4-6-0 No 73051 and BR Class 4 4-6-0 No 75073. Steaming at caution past the signalbox at Branksome in the summer of 1959 is SR U Class 2-6-0 No 31637, from 70C Guildford with a passenger train. (John Smith)

171) We linger for a while at Branksome, where, on 8th September 1962, SR Rebuilt *West Country* Class 4-6-2 No 34016 *Bodmin*, from 71A Eastleigh and looking in ex.works condition, tracks along light engine. Constructed in November 1945 and rebuilt at Eastleigh Works in April 1958, *Bodmin* also served from the sheds at 72A Exmouth Junction, 74B Ramsgate and 73A Stewarts Lane. Since withdrawal in June 1964 it has been actively preserved at the Mid-Hants Railway. (D.K.Jones)

172) By sheer coincidence the locomotive in this picture, BR Class 4 4-6-0 No 75027 also ended up as an active preserved item, this time on the Bluebell Railway after withdrawal from 10A Carnforth in August 1968. In April 1961, No 75027, from 82G Templecombe, heads tender-first towards Branksome sation. Note the soot-stained station canopies. During its short life, No 75027 also worked from a host of other sheds, including 81F Oxford and 10G Skipton. (A.C.Ingram)

173) And so we reach the end of the line at Bournemouth (West) where the upper quadrant signals in the foreground are firmly at danger. In the station, safety valves blowing, BR Class 4 2-6-0 No 76006 stands at the head of a rake of coaches sometime in 1963. No 76006 was allocated to Eastleigh from new in January 1953 and later served from Bournemouth (twice), Eastleigh (a further three times), Dorchester and Salisbury. It was withdrawn in July 1967. (N.L.Browne)

CHAPTER FOUR - LAST RITES ON THE SOMERSET AND DORSET

174) With rails already rusting from the lack of trains, LMS Class 8F 2-8-0 No 48706 (82F Bath Green Park) has only two days left to live as it departs from Evercreech Junction and heads for Bournemouth with a Great Western Society farewell to the S & D on 5th March 1966. So far as the author's knowledge extends, the S & D was one of the few major routes to remain 100% steam until the bitter end. On this note we come to the end of BR STEAMING IN THE SOUTH WEST. (N.E.Preedy)